LEADERS GUIDE

WHOSE MONEY IS IT?

M. E. MARSHALL

GRACE Publishing Incorporated
720 Moonlite Trce
Winder, GA. 30096

Ordering Information:
Quantity sales. Special discounts are available on quantity purchases by corporations, associations, and others. For details, contact the publisher at the address above.
Printed in the United States of America

Publisher's Cataloging-in-Publication data
Marshall, M.E.
Whose Money Is It? Leaders Guide - God Wants Your Heart Not Your Money
ISBN 978-0-9972576-5-6

1. The main category of the book —Faith Religion. 2. Finance —From one perspective.
First Edition

Table of Contents

Acknowledgements

Author's Preface

This Bible study workbook is truly a labor of love, beginning with a deep love for my Heavenly Father. It is also motivated by love for my brothers and sisters in Christ, as well as those who are searching for a better quality of life and may feel lost or overwhelmed. The experience of writing this book has been a journey, one for which I give all praise and gratitude to God. He has divinely orchestrated the events that ultimately led to the launching of G.R.A.C.E. Financial Ministry.

The Genesis of a Calling

The mission behind this study began many years ago in a small Baptist church in Georgia, located about 30 miles north of Atlanta. Having spent much of my career in the field of Credit and Collections, it seemed only natural that my first volunteer opportunity would be with the church's Finance Committee. I quickly realized I had a passion for this work, and soon found myself in a leadership position, responsible for managing the church's finances—a responsibility I took very seriously. I believe God placed a desire in my heart to be a faithful steward over His resources, and I served in this capacity for over thirteen years.

During those years, I witnessed many church members struggle with their finances. Sadly, I saw similar struggles among my colleagues in the secular workplace. It became apparent to me that both groups shared a common challenge: a misguided perspective on their resources. This realization inspired the formation of G.R.A.C.E. Financial Ministry—G.R.A.C.E. standing for God's Resources Advancing Christian Evangelism.

A Journey of Learning and Sharing

Over the years, I have attended numerous conferences, read many insightful books on finances, and facilitated small group studies, all of which deepened my understanding of what the Bible teaches about money, wealth, and stewardship. In addition to these experiences, I have researched the practical financial concerns and needs of individuals, especially as they relate to debt and money management.

My desire to share knowledge gained from both the secular world and spiritual teachings compelled me to write and develop this curriculum. My goal has always been to present these principles concisely that resonates with both Christians and non-Christians. The result is this Bible study, "Whose Money Is It?" My hope and prayer is that you are blessed by the material and that it offers a fresh perspective on God's resources.

Acknowledgements and Gratitude

I am deeply grateful for the support system that has held me accountable, encouraged, and challenged me along the way—especially my spiritual parents and friends, Pastor (Poppy) Erven and Jacquelyn Kimble. Pastor Kimble went home to be with the Lord on November 25, 2024. Under his mentorship, I learned how to study scripture to gain a true understanding of the truths in God's Word. He exposed me to the teachings of great leaders such as Tony Evans and John Maxwell, as well as ministries like Grace Ministries International and the North American Missions Board, among others.

While I cannot mention every individual or organization that has inspired and encouraged me, I sincerely acknowledge that I am a better person because of the influence of each one.

Introduction

Exploring Stewardship: Heart, Focus, Greed, Treasure, and Idols

Many reasons exist for why individuals sometimes fail to act responsibly in managing their time, talents, or treasures. This series highlights several significant factors that influence stewardship: the heart, focus, greed, treasure, and idols. Where a person stands in each of these areas ultimately determines whether they are acting as a good steward of God's gifts.

Session Structure and Approach

This five-part study is designed to be divided into five sessions, each consisting of two parts. Throughout the series, participants will encounter numerous scriptural references. Ample time should be devoted to meditating on each passage—a practice that will help participants memorize and internalize the truths found in God's Word.

Grasping the Concept: God as Owner, We as Managers

One of the initial subjects explored in the study is the concept that God is the owner of everything. Participants are challenged to reflect on what it means to be a steward or manager of someone else's property. This shift in perspective is essential to understanding true stewardship.

Reflecting on Time, Talent, and Treasures

Consider how your management of time, talent, and treasures reflects your stewardship. Have you ever realized that how you focus on these areas directly impacts your ability to manage the resources God has given you? Remember, God is the owner of everything—in the earth, on the earth, above the earth, and beyond.

Psalms 24:1-3 says, "T*he earth is the Lord's, and everything in it, the world, and all who live in it; for he founded it on the seas and established it on the waters. Who may ascend the mountain of the Lord? Who may stand in his holy place*?"

Stewardship Defined: Managers, Not Owners

Since everything belongs to the Lord, our role is not that of owners, but rather managers or stewards of what He has entrusted to us. A manager's responsibility is to oversee and care for property that does not belong to them. This perspective shifts the focus from possession to accountability and faithful administration of resources.

The Parable of the Talents: Responsibility According to Ability

Jesus illustrates this principle in the parable of the talents. In this story, a manager distributes talents—a significant amount of money, with one talent equaling approximately twenty years' wages for a day laborer—to his servants. Each servant receives a different amount, determined by their individual ability to handle the responsibility. The one entrusted with five talents is given a much greater responsibility compared to the servant who receives only one talent. This example highlights the importance of managing what God has given us faithfully, according to the abilities He has provided. Matthew 25:15 says: "*And to one he gave five talents, to another two, and to another one, to each according to his own ability; and immediately he went on a journey*."

God's Distribution of Resources: According to Our Abilities

The idea here is that God entrusts each of us with talents, time, or treasures based on our individual ability to manage them while we await His return. This means that the resources we possess are not distributed randomly, but rather in accordance with what God knows we are capable of handling. Just as in the parable, one servant is given five talents, another two, and another one—each allocation is intentional and matched to the recipient's abilities.

In verse 29, Jesus emphasizes the principle of stewardship and accountability: those who use what they have wisely will receive even more, while those who fail to steward their resources will lose even what they have. This underscores the importance of faithful management and the responsibility that comes with what God has entrusted to us. "*For to everyone who has, more will be given, and he will have abundance; but from him who does not have, even what he has will be taken away*."

The Source and Blessing of Wealth

Deuteronomy 8:18b clearly instructs us to "*remember the Lord your God, for it is he who gives you the ability to produce wealth*." This verse emphasizes that God not only created and owns all things, but He is also the one who grants us the capacity to acquire wealth. Our abilities and opportunities to gain material resources are gifts from Him, underscoring the importance of gratitude and dependence on God's provision.

Biblical Perspective: Wealth as a Blessing

Throughout both the Old and New Testaments, wealth is consistently portrayed as a blessing from God. Abraham serves as a prominent example of a God-fearing individual who was greatly blessed with material wealth, as noted in Genesis 13:2. The Psalmists, too, celebrate the material blessings bestowed upon the righteous. For instance, the godly person is described as flourishing "*like a tree planted by streams of water*" (Psalms 1:3), and it is declared that "*wealth and riches*" are found in the house of the individual who fears the Lord (Psalms 112:1, 3).

God's Generosity and Purpose for Wealth

God's generous nature is further highlighted in the New Testament, where Paul states that God "*richly furnishes us with everything to enjoy*" (1 Timothy 6:17). Material wealth, therefore, is seen as a consequence of God's bounty and goodness. These passages collectively affirm that all our resources originate from God, and any prosperity we experience should be recognized as a direct result of His kindness and provision.

So, let's see what hinders you from being a good manager!

Matters of the Heart

The Deceitfulness of the Human Heart

Scripture reveals the complexity and inherent deceitfulness of the human heart. As Jeremiah 17:9 states, "*The heart is deceitful above all things and beyond cure. Who can understand it*?" This verse highlights our limited ability to fully grasp or trust our own desires and motivations. The answer to this dilemma is found in God, who alone truly understands our hearts. Romans 8:27 affirms this truth: "*...he who searches our hearts knows the mind of the Spirit, because the Spirit intercedes for God's people in accordance with the will of God.*" God's intimate knowledge of our hearts assures us that He alone can guide us toward what is truly valuable and aligned with His will.

Assessing What We Value

Each of us must examine what we hold dear. What do you consider to be of value in your life? What are your heart's deepest desires? Is your love directed toward material possessions, social position, or the approval of others? These probing questions invite reflection and honesty, as they reveal the true priorities that govern our actions and decisions. Taking time to answer these questions is essential for understanding the state of our hearts.

The Danger of Loving Money

Scripture warns about the dangers of misplaced affection, especially the love of money. 1 Timothy 6:10 cautions, "*the love of money is the root to all kinds of evil.*" This warning is not about money itself, but the affection and priority given to it above all else. According to Matthew Henry's commentary, many are tempted to use their faith as a means of fulfilling earthly and secular desires. Henry points out that the principal Paul sets forth in 1 Timothy is "*godliness with contentment*" (1 Timothy 6:6). True spiritual fulfillment, therefore, comes not from the pursuit of material wealth but from cultivating a heart that is content and grounded in godliness.

Contrast with Worldly Success

This biblical perspective stands in stark contrast to the world's definition of success and accomplishment. While society often equates success with material gain, status, and recognition, Scripture encourages believers to seek spiritual contentment and godliness as the ultimate measure of a successful life. According to the dictionary, the definition of success is.

- The favorable and prosperous termination of attempts or endeavors
- The attainment of wealth, position, honors, or the like
- A successful performance or achievement
- A person or thing that is successful
- The accomplishment of an aim or purpose
- The attainment of popularity or profit

Jeff Haden, in his article "The Only Definition of Success That Matters," asserts that happiness is the true measure of success. This raises the question: Is happiness, as defined by contemporary standards, consistent with biblical principles? Furthermore, how does happiness differ from joy in a spiritual context? In Matthew 6:33, Jesus instructs his followers to "*seek first His kingdom and His righteousness, and all these things will be given to you as well.*" The "these things" refer to essential needs such as food, drink, and clothing, as discussed in the preceding parable about storing up treasures in Heaven. Jesus emphasizes prioritizing spiritual pursuits over material concerns, assuring that God will provide for those who trust in Him

The population faced significant hardship under Roman rule, enduring heavy taxation and widespread poverty. The arrival of the promised Messiah brought hope for freedom and relief from their difficult circumstances. Many were discouraged and longed for deliverance, especially as Judea's direct Roman administration, established in 4 BC, intensified tensions between the Jewish people and their rulers. They were ready to be rescued.

Jesus was not referring to material wealth, but to spiritual riches. He emphasized that while non-believers pursue material needs, those who have faith can trust that God will provide for them, just as He cares for the birds of the air. In Matthew 6:32b–33, Jesus assures, "*your heavenly Father knows that you need them. But seek first His kingdom and His righteousness, and all these things shall be added to you*".

Psalm 37:4 says *Take delight in the Lord, and he will give you the desires of your heart.* Wow, imagine that! Receiving the desires of your heart handed to you by the Most High, with His blessings!

So, what do we know? We know:

- The heart is deceitful.
- The love of money is the <u>root</u> to all kinds of evil.
- God searches and knows our heart.
- The world defines success in terms of gains, wealth, position, and popularity.
- Our Heavenly Father knows what we need.
- If we seek Him, He will supply all our needs.

The concept of joy, as referenced in scripture, is distinct from mere happiness. Proverbs 21:15 states, "*When justice is done, it brings joy to the righteous but terror to evildoers.*" Isaiah 12:3 describes joy as drawing water from the wells of salvation, signifying spiritual fulfillment. Paul, in Romans, encourages believers to be joyful in hope, patient in affliction, and faithful in prayer. Additionally, 3 John 1:4 expresses, "*I have no greater joy than to hear that my children are walking in the truth,*" John was talking about his spiritual children, those who received his testimony about Jesus and believed.

The dictionary defines joy as:

- The emotion of great delight or happiness caused by something exceptionally good or satisfying
- A source or cause of keen pleasure or delight
- The expression or display of glad feeling
- A state of happiness or felicity

But what about happiness, what does the dictionary say about that?

- The quality or state of being happy
- Good fortune; pleasure; contentment; joy

According to Webster's Dictionary, joy is defined as an **<u>emotion,</u>** while happiness is considered a **<u>state of mind.</u>** For example, John expressed his greatest joy in witnessing the positive impact of God's work in the lives of those he ministered to. Emotions, such as joy, are typically influenced by external circumstances; positive conditions foster positive emotions, while negative conditions can diminish them. Thus, by worldly standards, joy is conditional and subject to change.

Despite facing severe adversity, including imprisonment for casting out a "familiar spirit" from a female slave who proclaimed the living Christ, but only for a profit to her owners,

Paul and Silas responded by singing praises to the Lord. Their joy was not dependent on external circumstances but was rooted in their spiritual conviction. Roman prisons at the time were harsh environments—often underground, overcrowded, and unsanitary, with many prisoners suffering from disease, starvation, or abuse. Nevertheless, Paul and Silas demonstrated a positive response, exemplifying internal spiritual joy even in the most challenging conditions (see Acts 16:25).

Paul and Silas found joy in prison by focusing on their faith rather than their circumstances. Despite being unjustly imprisoned and enduring harsh conditions, they chose to sing praises to God. Their joy was not dependent on their external environment, which was miserable and oppressive, but was rooted in their spiritual conviction and trust in God. This internal, spiritual joy enabled them to respond positively, even in adversity, demonstrating that true joy comes from a relationship with God rather than from favorable circumstances.

Now let's turn our attention to happiness. The dictionary says happiness is a state of mind. Paul admonishes new Christians to "renew their minds". Romans 12:2; "*Do not conform to the pattern of this world, but be transformed by the renewing of your mind. Then you will be able to test and approve what God's will is—his good, pleasing and perfect will.*"

Having a renewed mind means embracing the perspective of Christ, as reflected in 1 Corinthians 2:16: "*For, who has known the mind of the Lord so as to instruct him? But we have the mind of Christ.*" So, what is the conclusion of the matter of the heart? Ultimately, God desires your heart rather than your material possessions. The foundation of this relationship is made possible through the life, death, and resurrection of His Son. Just as genuine love for another person inspires a desire to know and please them, so too should our love for God motivate us to seek a deeper relationship with Him.

Psalm 19:14 encapsulates this sentiment, emphasizing the importance of aligning our hearts with God. *"Let the words of my mouth and the meditation of my heart Be acceptable in Your sight, O Lord, my strength and my Redeemer".*

Your financial decisions are influenced by the relationship you cultivate with God through Jesus Christ. Personal worth is not determined by material possessions, but by the assurance of being loved by your Heavenly Father.

Prayer:
Heavenly Father,
Thank You for Your Word and for the guidance it provides. Help me to focus my heart and mind on You, to resist the distractions of this world, and to be transformed by the renewing of my mind. Grant me the strength and wisdom to put Your teachings into practice each day. May my life reflect Your love, truth, and purpose.
In Jesus' name, Amen.

Matters of the Heart – Bible Study Lesson

Introduction

Consider what you truly value and where your heart's desires lie. Is your affection directed toward material possessions, status, or the approval of others? As stated in 1 Timothy 6:10, "*the love of money is the root of all kinds of evil.*" Importantly, Paul does not claim that money itself is evil; rather, it is the value or allegiance placed on money that leads to harmful desires. Verse 9 further warns, "*But those who desire to be rich fall into temptation and a snare, and into many foolish and harmful lusts which drown men in destruction.*" For further reflection, read 1 Timothy 6:6–10.

According to Matthew Henry's commentary, the congregants were endeavoring to have their religion work for them AND their secular desires.

- What do you think Paul was trying to say?
- What do you value?
- What does society have to say about what is valuable?

Jeremiah 17:9 says "*The heart is deceitful above all things and beyond cure. Who can understand it*?" The New King James translation says 'wicked' as opposed to deceitful. The beginning of understanding whose money it is begins with the heart. What has your heart and/or who has your heart can determine how you make spending decisions. Jeremiah 17:1-10

1. Why is Jeremiah saying the heart is deceitful?

____
____
____

2. What do these verses say to you?

____
____
____

Read Romans 8:27

3. Does this verse answer Jeremiah's question?

____
____
____

4. How would you respond?

____
____
____

5. Does being happy equal being content?

____
____
____

6. Does joy come with happiness, or is it based on something more significant?

Read 3 John 1:4

7. Who is talking in this passage? Who is the audience?

Read Psalm 37:4

8. What does this verse say should be your priority?

When you think about joy, what comes to mind? Joy is defined, by Webster's, as an emotion but what is joy according to the Bible?

Read Act 16:25

9. Based on the circumstances, would you have joy?

10. Fill in the heart below. The outer rim reflects what you show to others, the next inner layer is what your family and friends see, and the center reflects your relationship with God, your 'Heart'.

Color in Your Heart

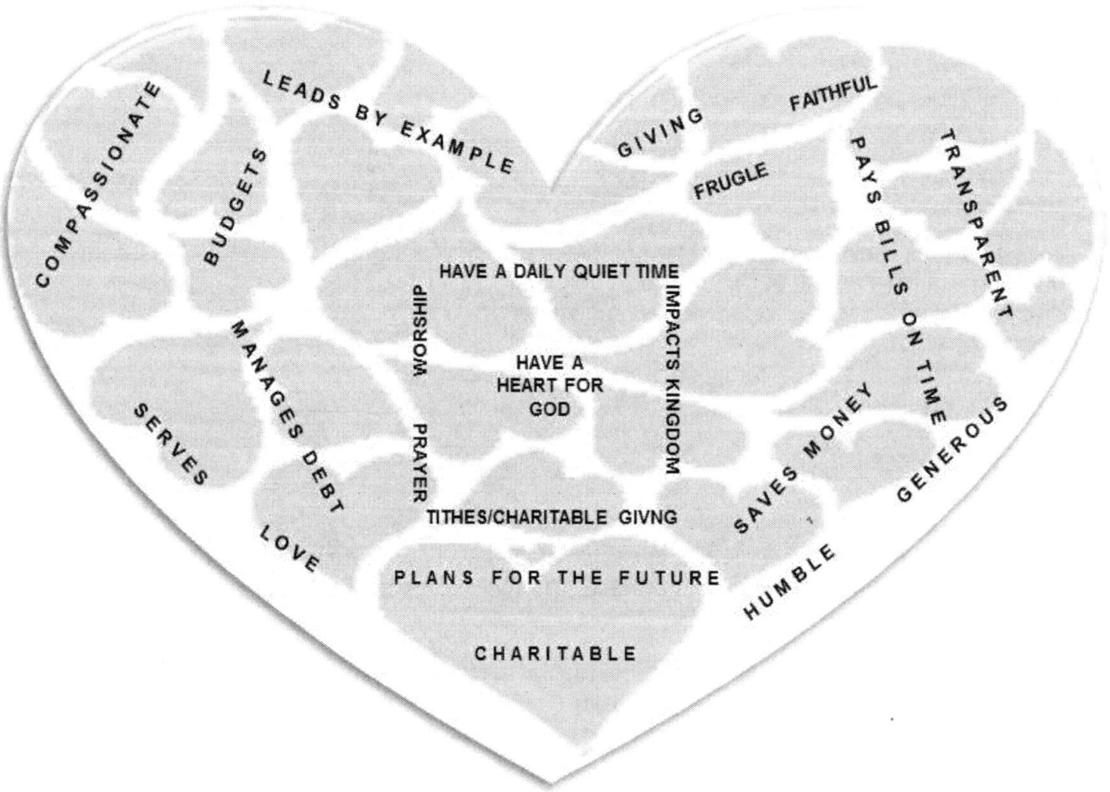

What's Your Focus?

Consider what occupies your thoughts throughout the day and where your attention is focused. Is it work-related tasks, upcoming events, or commitments at your local church? Whatever it may be, your focus often centers on a single priority. In Psalm 86, David, the author, admonishes the Lord to hear him and acknowledges his need. He asks the Lord for an undivided heart, (some translations say "unite my heart) seeking to remain steadfast in his relationship with God. Despite being anointed as the future king of Israel, David experienced a period of waiting before assuming the throne, during which his focus remained on being in right standing with God.

David's Journey and Focus Amid Trials

David was still a young man, just 20 years old, when he achieved a remarkable victory by defeating Goliath. Despite this accomplishment, his life was soon overshadowed by the actions of King Saul. Saul, driven by insecurity, disobedience, and jealousy, turned against David and actively sought to take his life. This period of David's life was marked by constant danger and uncertainty as he fled from Saul's relentless pursuit.

According to The New Bible Dictionary Third Edition, "Once Saul was dead, David sought the will of God and was guided to return to Judah, his own tribal region. Here his fellow-tribesmen anointed him king, and he took up royal residence in Hebron. He was then 30 years old… David's long reign was to last for 33 years." (Jones, T. H)

Even after becoming king in Hebron, David's challenges were far from over. He experienced additional hardship when he had to flee from Absalom, his own son, who sought to overthrow him. Throughout these trials—whether being hunted by Saul or later by Absalom—David had every reason to be consumed by his own difficulties and personal struggles. If anyone had justification to focus solely on themselves and their problems, it would have been David. Yet, his story demonstrates a continual seeking after God and a desire to remain steadfast, even amid adversity.

Daily Distractions and Competing Priorities

In today's high-tech world, there are countless distractions vying for your attention. Even those closest to you—your friends, family, and children—can unintentionally pull you away from spending meaningful time with God. Beyond personal relationships, technology plays a significant role in diverting your focus. Smartphones, tablets, laptops, AI and social media platforms are all designed to keep your attention on things other than God.

Distractions begin the moment you wake up. If you turn on the morning news, advertisers immediately compete for your attention, promoting everything from aspirin to Zumba classes. While commuting, the radio offers another stream of information, with talk show hosts discussing the latest celebrity gossip or political events. They share their perspectives and even invite listeners to contribute their own 'expert' opinions. Local and national news stories often evoke concern or alarm, leaving you to wonder what is truly happening in the world today.

Workplace Distractions and Divided Attention

Once you arrive at work, it's easy to get caught up in distractions that fill your mind with various topics and concerns. The familiar "water cooler" conversation often centers around last night's ball game, the latest drama on popular TV shows like "Housewives," or other trending entertainment. These casual discussions, while seemingly harmless, compete for your attention and occupy your thoughts.

In addition to these conversations, the day is further fragmented by the constant influx of e-mails, the demands of video conferencing, especially if you work from home and other idle exchanges with coworkers. These activities, though part of the daily routine, contribute to a cluttered mind, making it difficult to focus on what truly matters. With so many things vying for your attention, it becomes challenging to set aside time to reflect on the things of God.

This divided attention raises important questions: When do you intentionally make space to think about spiritual matters and your relationship with God? Why is your focus so often split among so many competing interests? Romans 8:5-6 addresses this struggle, reminding us of the contrast between a mind set on worldly distractions and one governed by the Spirit, which leads to life and peace.

> *"Those who live according to the flesh have their minds set on what the flesh desires; but those who live in accordance with the Spirit have their minds set on what the Spirit desires. The mind governed by the flesh is death, but the mind governed by the Spirit is life and peace."*

An Illustration of Distraction: Brownie's Story

I had a female lab/shepherd mix named Brownie. When she was nine years old, she weighed approximately 80 pounds but still behaved as if she were a puppy weighing only 20 pounds. Brownie, in my opinion, exhibited her own form of Attention Deficit Disorder (ADD). I say this because whenever I took her outside to relieve herself, she was easily distracted by every little thing around her. Whether it was another dog passing by, a squirrel darting through the yard, a gust of wind, or even a sudden sound, any minor stimulus would quickly capture her attention.

It didn't take much for Brownie to lose focus on the task at hand. Once distracted, it often took her a moment to regain her composure and remember the original reason she was outside. This tendency to become sidetracked serves as a relatable example of how easy it is for any of us to get off track, especially when surrounded by constant distractions.

Spiritual Distraction: A Detour in Direction (ADD)

Many Christians, much like the story of Brownie, experience their own kind of distraction, which can be described as "A Detour in Direction" (ADD)—not the clinical diagnosis, but rather a spiritual tendency to lose focus. God has a specific plan and a set of requirements for each of us, as outlined in Jeremiah 29:11. Despite these clear intentions, it is easy to become sidetracked and stray from the path God has set.

A fitting example comes from the book of Exodus, where the Israelites repeatedly disobeyed God's commands. In chapter 16, when the people requested food, God provided manna from heaven. He gave precise instructions on how much manna to collect each day. However, some gathered more than necessary, whether from a lack of faith or out of greed. As a result, the excess manna spoiled by the next day and was no longer suitable to eat—they expected it to remain fresh until they wanted it.

Exodus 16:28 records God's response: "*Then the Lord said to Moses, 'How long will you refuse to keep my commands and my instructions*?'" This question reflects God's concern over the persistent pattern of distraction and disobedience among His people. Just as the Israelites struggled to remain attentive to God's guidance, we too can easily get off track and lose sight of His direction for our lives.

A Call to Obedience: Recognizing God's Commands

The same challenge that faced the Israelites in the wilderness is relevant to us today: How long will we continue to neglect acknowledging God and keeping His commandments? This is a question of priority and devotion, as God calls His people to faithfulness in all areas of life, including the stewardship of their resources.

The Principle of the Tithe

One of God's clear instructions is the command to give a tenth of all increase—a tithe—back to Him, as referenced in Malachi 3:8. Importantly, the practice of tithing did not originate with the Mosaic Law nor is it exclusive to the Old Testament. Its roots can be traced back to Abraham, who, in gratitude for victory, offered a tenth of the goods he had gained in battle. This act of thankfulness and obedience is recorded in Genesis 14:18-20.

Spiritual Tools for Obedience

The apostle Paul, in 2 Corinthians 10:5-6, equips believers with the spiritual tools necessary for obedience. Through Paul's guidance, we learn how to bring our thoughts and actions in alignment with God's will, empowering us to live obedient and focused lives. *"We demolish arguments and every pretension that sets itself up against the knowledge of God, and we take captive every thought to make it obedient to Christ. And we will be ready to punish every act of disobedience, once your obedience is complete".*

You are to take captive every thought, and I would also suggest every deed. The dictionary's definition for captive is.

- A person who is enslaved or dominated
- Made or held prisoner
- Kept in confinement or restraint
- Pertaining to a captive.

The Nature of Our Thoughts and Staying Focused on God

There are many types of thoughts that can be considered good. Inspirational messages from co-workers or acquaintances, and even spam emails, are received almost every day. People encounter funny thoughts, motivational quotes, daily reflections, and positive ideas regularly. While none of these are inherently bad, it is important to recognize their place in our lives.

Proverbs 12:15 offers wisdom on this matter: "*The way of a fool is right in his own eyes, but he who listens to counsel is wise.*" According to Webster's dictionary, a fool is defined as a person who lacks judgment or sense. This reminds us that not all thoughts, even those that seem good, lead to wisdom unless they are guided by sound counsel.

It is easy to lose focus on the things of God. The questions arise: why does this happen? Why do some people put God aside, perhaps only considering Him on Sundays, if at all? The Old Testament recounts that after the Israelites were delivered from Pharaoh by Moses, God gave them the Law. In Deuteronomy 11:18, it is written, "*Fix these words of mine in your hearts and minds; tie them as symbols on your hands and bind them on your foreheads.*" In this passage, the words "hearts" and "minds" are central. While the heart has been discussed earlier, it is now important to consider the mind and its role in maintaining focus on God.

Going back to Webster's, mind is defined as.

- The element, part, substance, or process that; reasons, thinks, feels, wills, perceives, judges, etc.: "the processes of the human mind."

- Psychology - The totality of conscious and unconscious mental processes and activities.
- Intellect or understanding, as distinguished from the faculties of feeling and will, intelligence.
- Reason, sanity, or sound mental condition

The Role of the Mind in Focusing on God

The mind serves as the essential part of the body that empowers us to reason, think, feel, and choose. It is through the mind that we process information, make decisions, and form judgments. Considering the scripture from Deuteronomy, we are encouraged to "fix"—that is, to make a conscious decision to focus our minds on God's words. This means intentionally directing our attention toward the teachings of the Bible and allowing these truths to guide our thoughts and actions.

Implementing this focus requires more than passive listening. As James 1:22 instructs, "*Do not merely listen to the word, and so deceive yourselves. Do what it says.*" In other words, it is not enough to simply hear or read the Word; we must also put it into practice. This active engagement with scripture helps us maintain our focus on God, shaping our minds and lives according to His will.

James encourages believers to move beyond merely hearing or reading the Word, urging them to put it into practice. This requires intentional focus and disciplined effort, which cannot be achieved if one allows worldly distractions to dominate their thoughts. Paul reinforces this in Romans 12:2: "*And do not be conformed to this world, but be transformed by the renewing of your mind, that you may prove what is that good and acceptable and perfect will of God.*" To be conformed is to imitate, follow, adapt, or obey prevailing norms. In contrast, Paul calls Christians to be transformed—altered and renewed—rather than simply blending in. Ultimately, believers are called to be nonconformists, refusing to accept the ideologies of this world and instead embracing the principles of God's kingdom.

Commit today to intentionally renew your mind and align your actions with God's Word. Set aside time to reflect, eliminate distractions, and actively pursue transformation, so that your life reflects the values and purpose to which you are called

What's Your Focus? - Bible Study Lesson

Introduction
The Example of David's Focused Heart

In Psalm 86, David prays specifically for an undivided heart. Despite facing many distractions, David ultimately recognized that what he chose to focus on had a significant impact on his life. Although he was anointed at a young age, many years passed before he actually became king over Israel. Throughout this period, David had numerous opportunities to let his circumstances, personal challenges, or inner struggles consume his attention. However, his prayer and example demonstrate the importance of directing one's mind toward God, regardless of external situations.

- What do you think about during the day?
- What thoughts occupy your mind?
- What has your undivided attention?

There are so many distractions in the high-tech world we live in today. So, when do we think about the things of God? What can you do to stay focused on God?

Read Romans 8:5-6

1. What does this scripture say to you about what should be your focus?

____
____
____

Christians tend to suffer from ADD and get off focus, A Detour in Direction. God has a plan for each of us, and He has commands and requirements for us. In Exodus, the Israelite continued to disobey the Lord's commands, He gave specific instructions for gathering manna each day. The people, out of a lack of faith or greed, gathered more than they should, it was spoiled the next day.

Read Exodus 16:16

2. Do you think the Israelites had a spiritual ADD (*A Detour in Direction*)?

____
____
____

Read 2 Corinthians 10:5

3. In order to take your thoughts captive, what must you do?

____
____
____

Read Proverbs 12:15

4. Does thinking good thoughts alone, allow you to take every thought & make it obedient to Christ?

5. Ok, so you know you get off focus on the things of God, but now the question is why?

6. Why do you sometimes put God on the back burner, and maybe only think about Him on Sunday's if at all?

Read Deuteronomy 11:18

Two key words in this text that stand out are "hearts" and "minds". Basically, the mind is the part of the body that allows human beings to reason, think, feel, will etc. And according to our scripture from Deuteronomy, we are to fix or make a conscience decision to focus on God's Words, or His 'Word", which is the Bible and its teachings.

7. What prevents you from focusing on God's Word?

Read Colossians 3:1-3

8. What is Paul saying here?

Read Romans 12:2

9. What does be conformed mean? What are some examples of how you conform to this world?

10. What will you do to keep your mind focused on the things of God?

Read 2 Chronicles 7:14

11. What does this passage say to you?

Is Greed Good or Bad?

In the 1987 film *Wall Street*, Michael Douglas's character, Gordon Gekko, famously declared, "Greed, for lack of a better word, is good. Greed is right, greed works. Greed clarifies, cuts through, and captures the essence of the evolutionary spirit. Greed, in all of its forms—greed for life, for money, for love, knowledge—has marked the upward surge of mankind." Gekko's statement suggests that ambition and the drive to achieve more can be healthy, motivating individuals to pursue advancement and success. However, this "whatever it takes" mentality raises important questions about the role of motivation and the desires of the heart in shaping our actions and values.

What Does the Bible Say About Greed?

The Bible addresses the topic of greed in multiple passages, offering clear guidance on its dangers and consequences. Psalm 10:3 states, "*For the wicked boasts of his heart's desire; He blesses the greedy and renounces the Lord.*" This verse highlights how those who are greedy often prioritize their own desires above their relationship with God, ultimately turning away from Him.

Proverbs 1:19 further warns, "*Such are the paths of all who go after ill-gotten gain; it takes away the life of those who get it.*" Here, the pursuit of dishonest gain is shown to have destructive effects, robbing individuals of true life and fulfillment.

Additionally, in 1 Timothy 3:3, one of the qualifications for church leadership is that a person should be "*not given to wine, not violent, not greedy for money, but gentle, not quarrelsome, not covetous.*" This requirement underscores how greed is incompatible with the character expected of spiritual leaders, emphasizing the importance of self-control and contentment.

Through these passages, it is evident that the Bible speaks extensively about greed—addressing its root causes, warning against its dangers, and outlining the negative outcomes for those who allow greed to guide their actions.

Curiously, Webster's definition is limited.

- Excessive or rapacious desire, especially for wealth or possessions

Understanding the Nature of Rapacious Greed

Rapacious is certainly an SAT word. Its definition— "inordinately greedy, predatory; extortionate"—aptly characterizes individuals who relentlessly pursue their own gain, often at the expense of others. This description fits Gordon Gekko from the film Wall Street, whose insatiable appetite for wealth and power epitomizes rapacious behavior.

Other synonyms for rapacious include greedy, voracious, gluttonous, ravenous, and insatiable. Each term conveys a sense of excessive desire that goes beyond normal ambition; instead, it points to an unrestrained and unhealthy craving for more, regardless of the consequences to oneself or others. Unlike Gekko's articulate justification of greed, these words paint a picture of something much less noble—crudely selfish and self-serving.

This understanding of greed stands in stark contrast to the teachings of the Bible. While popular culture may sometimes glamorize greed, scripture emphasizes the importance of self-denial. Jesus instructs His followers that to truly follow Him, one must deny oneself, rejecting selfishness and placing the needs of others—and obedience to God—above personal desires.

In Matthew 16:24 Jesus says. "*If anyone desires to come after Me, let him deny himself, and take up his cross, and follow Me".* In 1 John 2:15 Jesus also says. *"Do not love the world or anything in the world. If anyone loves the world, love for the Father is not in them."*John 12:25 puts it this way. *"Anyone who loves their life will lose it, while anyone who hates their life in this world will keep it for eternal life."*

The Biblical Perspective on Greed and Its Consequences

The Bible addresses the issue of greed, emphasizing that it impacts not only a person's life in the present but also their eternal destiny. According to scripture, greed is considered wicked and has serious implications for one's spiritual standing. In fact, the Bible states that greed can disqualify an individual from serving as a Pastor or Deacon, highlighting the severity of its consequences within the faith community.

This raises the question: why do some people become greedy, selfish, or both? Characters like Mr. Gekko exemplify an extreme pursuit of wealth and power, stopping at nothing to achieve their desires. However, for the average person, the motivation for greed—whether for wealth or possessions—can often be traced back to having the wrong perspective. When individuals derive their sense of value and worth from people or material possessions instead of from God and His redemptive work through His Son on the Cross, they become vulnerable to the trap of greed.

The Roots of Human Selfishness and Greed

Human beings, due to our inherent sinful nature, are naturally inclined toward selfishness. This tendency is well captured by the British poet Samuel Butler, who remarked, "Self-preservation is the first law of nature." Building on this idea, it could be argued that if self-preservation is indeed the primary instinct, then greed follows closely as the second. Both self-preservation and greed are evident throughout human history and experience.

Self-Preservation in the Garden of Eden

The earliest scriptural example of self-preservation appears in the account of the Garden of Eden. After Adam and Eve ate from the forbidden tree, Adam attempted to shift responsibility by saying, "The woman whom You gave to be with me, she gave me of the tree, and I ate" (Genesis 3:12). In turn, the woman blamed the serpent. Despite these efforts to avoid accountability, all parties were ultimately held responsible for their actions, and each suffered the resulting consequences that continue to affect humanity to this day.

The Destructive Impact of Greed

Greed has been responsible for the breakdown of families, the collapse of major corporations, the downfall of countries and states, and, most significantly, the loss of the human soul. One of the most significant consequences of greed is its effect on family relationships. The leading reported cause of divorce is money. As noted in an article from the Huffington Post by Sonya Britt, a researcher at Kansas State University, "Arguments about money [are] by far the top predictor of divorce." She emphasizes that it is not children, sex, in-laws, or any other issue, but money that leads to the dissolution of marriages for both men and women.

Further supporting this view, Jeffrey Dew, co-author of the article, points out that "arguments about money may also stem from couples' deeply held beliefs about the purpose of money." The use of the phrase "deeply held beliefs" highlights the fact that financial disagreements are often rooted in fundamental differences in values and perspectives regarding money. These underlying conflicts can create lasting rifts within families, ultimately leading to dysfunction and separation.

The Demands of Modern Life and Their Impact on Family

All too often, both men and women find themselves working 80-hour weeks, which leaves little opportunity to spend quality time with their families—especially their children. In today's highly technical world, we are constantly surrounded by devices and tools such as smartphones, tablets, laptops, video conferencing, Bluetooth, and Skype, all designed to keep us connected and always in the proverbial loop. While these technologies are intended to increase our productivity and connectivity, they often contribute to the reduction of meaningful family interactions.

A Cultural Reflection: "The Cat's in the Cradle"

A song from the 1960s, "The Cat's in the Cradle" sung by Harry Chapin, poignantly captures the consequences of this imbalance. The lyrics tell a sad but telling story about the relationship between a father and his son, highlighting how work and other obligations can lead to missed moments and distant relationships within families.

My child arrived just the other day
He came to the world in the usual way
But there were planes to catch and bills to pay
He learned to walk while I was away
And he was talkin' 'fore I knew it, and as he grew
He'd say "I'm gonna be like you, Dad
You know I'm gonna be like you"

There are more verses, but the ending verses say a lot about the example we can leave for our children.

I've long since retired, my son's moved away
I called him up just the other day
I said, "I'd like to see you if you don't mind"
He said, "I'd love to, Dad, if I can find the time
You see my new job's a hassle and kids have the flu
But it's sure nice talking to you, Dad
It's been sure nice talking to you"
And as I hung up the phone it occurred to me
He'd grown up just like me
My boy was just like me

The Legacy We Leave: Lessons for Our Children and Corporate Downfalls

As parents, it is crucial to reflect on the legacy we are passing on to our children. The behaviors and values we display set a powerful example for the next generation. Are we demonstrating that family relationships and togetherness matter most, or are we, perhaps unintentionally, showing that the pursuit of wealth and material gain takes precedence over family bonds? The choices we make and the priorities we set will inevitably influence our children's understanding of what is truly important in life.

The destructive impact of greed is not limited to personal relationships or families—it extends to the business world as well. Numerous major corporations have collapsed under the weight of their leaders' unchecked greed. Notable among these is the infamous Enron scandal. Enron's executives were found guilty of inflating the company's revenue by $586 million between 1997 and 2001. According to The New York Times, the company went so far as to allocate $1.5 million for its 2001 Christmas party. Employees enjoyed extravagant perks, including free laptops, catered office lunches at Houston's (an exclusive restaurant), lavish vacations, and even luxury cars. The prevailing atmosphere suggested that no expense was spared; the sky was the limit. However, behind this façade of prosperity lay deception and excess, driven by greed.

Ultimately, the illusion collapsed, resulting in the downfall of the company and devastating consequences for countless employees and stakeholders.

The Effects of Greed on the Human Soul

When considering the deeper spiritual impact of greed, it is important to reflect on how it affects an individual's soul. In Luke 11:39, Jesus addresses this issue directly, saying, "*Now you Pharisees make the outside of the cup and dish clean, but your inward part is full of greed and wickedness.*" His words reveal that the Pharisees were primarily concerned with outward appearances and how they were perceived by others, rather than focusing on the internal matters that truly matter to God. Their motivations and hearts were corrupted by greed, highlighting a disconnect between external actions and internal spiritual health. The term "Pharisee" itself is rooted in the Aramaic word פרש (prsh), meaning "to separate, divide, or distinguish." This origin underscores their tendency to set themselves apart, often emphasizing ritual and appearance over genuine devotion.

The Biblical Warning Against Greed

To revisit 1 Timothy 6:10: "*For the love of money is a root of all kinds of evil, for which some have strayed from the faith in their greediness, and pierced themselves through with many sorrows.*" This passage underscores the serious consequences of misplaced priorities—straying from faith and experiencing deep sorrow. According to the Asbury Bible Commentary, Paul's intent is to characterize the opponents of the Gospel and address the confusion between genuine godliness and the pursuit of financial gain.

The warning in 1 Timothy 6:10 about the love of money leading to all kinds of evil is highly relevant today. In modern society, the pursuit of wealth and material success is often equated with personal value and achievement. This mindset can lead individuals to prioritize financial gain over integrity, relationships, and even their spiritual well-being.

Applying This Principle in Our Lives Today

Many people experience pressure to "keep up" with societal standards, sometimes compromising their values or straying from their faith in the process. The passage's caution about being "pierced with many sorrows" is reflected in the stress, anxiety, and dissatisfaction that can result from an excessive focus on money. Additionally, as the Asbury Bible Commentary notes, confusing godliness with financial gain remains a challenge—some may believe that prosperity is a sign of spiritual favor, which can distort true faith. Ultimately, this scripture encourages a balanced perspective: to view money as a tool rather than a measure of worth, and to seek contentment and purpose beyond material possessions.

Is Greed Good or Bad? - Bible Study Lesson

Introduction
Understanding the Roots of Greed

Greed often raises the question of its true origins. Is it simply the result of an earnest desire for success and recognition that has taken a negative turn? Or does it have deeper roots in our inherent sin nature, materialism, and selfishness? These questions invite us to reflect on our motivations and the ways in which the pursuit of achievement can become distorted.

The ideals famously expressed by the character Gordon Gekko in the film Wall Street continue to resonate in various forms, even decades after the movie's release. His message about greed being "good" is still echoed in modern culture, prompting us to examine our own attitudes toward wealth and ambition.

Considering where we each stand on the "greed meter" offers an opportunity to compare ourselves not only with contemporary society but also with the people in Jesus' time. This reflection helps highlight the enduring relevance of the issue and encourages honest evaluation of our personal values and priorities.

Read Matthew 19:15-22

1. Based on this chapter, how would you say the young man felt about wealth?

____
____
____
____

Read Matthew 19:23

2. Why did Jesus say it was hard for a rich person to enter the kingdom of Heaven?

____
____
____

Read Luke 12:13-19

3. Jesus is asked to help with an inheritance. How would you describe the mindset of the man wanting his brother to divide the inheritance?

____
____
____

4. How would you define the rich man in this parable?

____
____
____

5. Have you ever had thoughts like the rich man or the brother wanting to split the inheritance?

____
____

Read Luke 12:16-20

6. In this story, the rich man was greedy for more. What were the consequences of his greed and what does God say about the man's actions?

Read 1 Timothy 6:6-10

7. There is a saying, the one with the most toys wins the game, but is that really true? What are your thoughts on what makes you content? Is it internal or external?

Read Proverbs 23:17

8. Society today puts a value on what a person wears, the car they drive, or house or neighborhood where they live. It is likely there are many wealthy people who are not believers and live very extravagant lives. With the light of Proverbs 23:17 shining on the lives of much of the wealthy, would you say envy is one cause of greed?

Read Ecclesiastes 5:13

9. Solomon, the wisest and richest man in the world implies wealth can cause the owner harm. How did it cause him harm? Has money caused you harm and in what way?

10. Do you have to be rich for money to cause harm?

What Do You Treasure?

Understanding True Treasure

When you think of treasure, what comes to mind? For many, the image is of chests brimming with gold coins and sparkling jewelry, reminiscent of pirates, boats, Captain Hook, and eye patches. While this imagery may not resonate with everyone, it's clear that treasure is typically associated with something of great value.

There are numerous passages in the Bible that reference 'treasure.' In fact, the King James Version mentions the word 'treasure' seventy-eight times. The term is used in various contexts, referring to money, affection, possessions, and other things of value. Notably, Jesus described the "Kingdom of Heaven" as a treasure. His teachings often began with illustrative comparisons: "The Kingdom of Heaven is like… a treasure hidden in a field… a man who sowed good seed in his field… a mustard seed… a merchant searching for fine pearls," and so on.

Through these teachings, Jesus emphasizes an important truth about treasures: while the world may focus on material wealth and possessions, true treasure is spiritual, not physical. The real value lies in the things that are eternal and rooted in faith, rather than the fleeting riches of this world.

Seeking True Treasures

The 'treasures' we are to seek are found in the things of God, not in material possessions. While the world often defines treasure as something tangible—such as wealth, expensive items, or physical assets—true treasure goes beyond what can be held or owned. The value of treasure can be found in moments we cherish, memorable experiences that shape us, and meaningful relationships that enrich our lives.

Treasure does not have to be limited to something of monetary worth or physical form. The moments we treasure, the experiences that leave a lasting impact, and the relationships we build are all significant forms of treasure. These are rooted in the spiritual, emotional, and relational aspects of life, rather than the fleeting nature of material possessions.

Let's look at a definition of treasure:

- Wealth or riches stored or accumulated, especially in the form of precious metals, money, jewels, or plate.
- Anything or person greatly valued or highly prized
- To regard or treat as precious; cherish.
- To put away for security or future use, as money

God's Definition of Treasure vs. Ours

Does your definition of treasure differ from God's? The Bible provides clear examples of how God defines treasure, which often contrasts with our human understanding focused on material possessions and wealth.

Israelites as God's Special Treasure

In the book of Exodus, God rescued the Israelites from slavery under Pharaoh in Egypt, using Moses as His chosen deliverer. In Exodus 19:5, God speaks to His people through Moses, declaring, "*Now therefore, if you will indeed obey My voice and keep My covenant, then you shall be a special treasure to Me above all people; for all the earth is Mine.*" This emphasizes the profound value God places on His people, considering them a "special treasure" above all others. Imagine being treasured by the Creator of all things—not because of material wealth, but because of obedience and relationship.

Job's Perspective on Treasure

Job's declaration— "I *have not departed from the commandment of His lips; I have treasured the words of His mouth More than my necessary food*," reflects a profound spiritual truth. Job is expressing that his commitment to God's instructions and teachings is more vital to him than even the basic sustenance required for physical survival.

This prioritization reveals several key insights:

- **Spiritual Nourishment Over Physical Needs:** Job places the value of God's Word above his daily bread, emphasizing that spiritual obedience and connection to God are more essential than material or physical needs.
- **Obedience as True Treasure:** For Job, true wealth is found in faithfully following God's commandments. His "treasure" is not in possessions or status, but in the relationship and alignment with God's will
- **Perspective on Value:** This attitude challenges readers to consider what they truly value. Is it material comfort, or is it the wisdom and guidance found in scripture? Job's example encourages us to reflect on our own priorities and to seek a deeper relationship with God, where His Word becomes our greatest treasure.

The Biblical View of Treasure: Time, Talent, and Wealth

In church settings, the term "treasure" is most associated with money. However, the Christian understanding of treasure encompasses far more than financial resources. Believers are encouraged to dedicate not only their material wealth but also their time and talents to advance the gospel of Jesus Christ. This holistic stewardship means that while treasure does include wealth, money, or anything of value, these are not negative in themselves.

Scripture affirms that wealth itself is a gift from God. In Deuteronomy 8:18a, it is stated, "*And you shall remember the Lord your God, for it is He who gives you power to get wealth*." This acknowledgment reframes wealth: it is not inherently bad, since its ultimate source is God. The blessings and resources we possess are entrusted to us by Him.

Importantly, the purpose of these treasures is not solely for personal gain, even though personal benefit often results. Rather, God provides these resources so that they may be used in service to others. This perspective encourages Christians to view their possessions, abilities, and time as tools for ministry and acts of love, rather than ends in themselves.

The Danger of Misplaced Treasure

People often encounter challenges when material treasures begin to overshadow their relationship with Christ and their service to Him. The teachings of Jesus, as recorded in Matthew 6:21 and Luke 12:34, make this clear: "For where your treasure is, there your heart will be also." This timeless principle asks us to consider what truly holds our affection and devotion.

Reflecting on What We Value

This lesson began with a simple yet profound question: "When you think of treasure, what comes to mind?" This prompts us to reflect deeply—do we value friends, family, reputation, social status, position, or is our highest priority our relationship with the Most High God? What we cherish most reveals the true orientation of our hearts.

The Focus of Stewardship

The central aim of this series is to emphasize the importance of being a good steward of all that God provides. In this context, treasures certainly include money, possessions, and other items of monetary value. However, their significance is only meaningful in relation to our Godly focus. The real question becomes: how do our resources and treasures align with and reflect our commitment to God?

Applying God-Focused Stewardship in Modern Life

King David's Example of Spiritual Focus
In the "What's Your Focus" lesson, King David is highlighted as an example of someone whose primary concern was maintaining a right relationship with the God of the Universe. His life illustrates how spiritual priorities can guide a person's choices and actions, especially regarding material blessings.

Monetary Resources in Contemporary Society
Translating this principle to today's society, consider the scenario of being blessed with a spacious four-bedroom house. Features such as large rooms, elegant crown molding, hardwood floors throughout the main level, a generous master suite, and a sizeable backyard with a wraparound deck and BBQ pit provide ample comfort and space for guests.

Stewardship Beyond Personal Enjoyment
If your focus is on God, you recognize that these blessings are not solely for personal enjoyment. Instead, your home becomes a resource for ministry and fellowship. Hosting Small Group Bible studies or inviting friends, family, or colleagues for a barbecue offers opportunities for others to witness how a godly home and family interact. Through hospitality and genuine relationships, your home serves as a space for Christian witnessing and encouragement. Depending on God's call on your life and He does have a call on your life as it says in Jeremiah 29:11, *"For I know the plans I have for you, declares the Lord, plans to prosper you and not to harm you, plans to give you hope and a future."* In Ephesians 1:11 is says
"In him we were also chosen, having been predestined according to the plan of him who worksout everything in conformity with the purpose of his will…"

God's Purposeful Plans and Our Response

Through the scriptures, it becomes clear that God communicates His intentions for our lives—He assures us that He has a plan, and those plans are carefully designed to align with the greater purposes of His will. This understanding leaves no room for selfishness or greed in the way we live. Instead, our focus should shift from personal gain to fulfilling God's purposes, trusting that His direction leads to hope and a meaningful future. By surrendering our own desires, we allow God's plans to unfold, ensuring that our actions are guided by His will rather than self-interest. Jesus told His disciples in Mathew 28:19 *"Therefore go and make disciples of all nations, baptizing them in the name of the Father and of the Son and of the Holy Spirit, and teaching them to obey everything I have commanded you. And surely I am with you always, to the very end of the age."*

Everyday Opportunities for Testimony

In our modern world, opportunities to share our faith are closer than we might think. We do not need to travel far; often, the chance to witness is as near as the house next door, the adjacent office or cubicle, or even within our own households. We are cautioned by Peter in 1 Peter 3:15 *"Always be prepared to give an answer to everyone who asks you to give the reason for the hope that you have. But do this with gentleness and respect…*" This sounds like giving a testimony to me.

Practical Ways to Share Your Testimony and Bless Others

It is understandable to feel hesitant about opening your home to strangers. In such cases, consider reaching out to unsaved friends, family members, or co-workers. Sharing your testimony is simply telling your personal story of what God has accomplished in your life.

God has entrusted you with resources—your treasures—not only for your own benefit but also to help fulfill His purposes. For example, your vehicle can be used to deliver food or clothing to local shelters or community cooperatives, providing tangible support to those in need.

Additionally, take time to look through your closets. Items such as old suits, shoes, dresses, and slacks can be donated to organizations that assist individuals re-entering the workforce or those who are underemployed and in need of appropriate business attire. By sharing what you have, you extend generosity and help others take meaningful steps forward. You truly are blessed to be a blessing; and also, be a witness and a light in a dark world.

What Do You Treasure? – Bible Study Lesson

Introduction
The Connection Between Treasure and Heart

Jesus taught, "*Where your treasure is, your heart will be also.*" This statement invites us to examine what we truly value and to consider how our priorities shape our lives. It's worth asking ourselves: do we really believe that what we value has our heart?

For example, if you highly value your car, does that mean your heart belongs to your car? At first glance, this idea seems almost absurd. After all, a car is just an object. But it's not the physical car itself that captures our affections—it's what the car represents. Owning a particular car might symbolize status or success and can even spark feelings of envy among friends and family.

Ultimately, the issue goes deeper than attachment to material things. It's not about developing a "love affair" with an inanimate object. Rather, it's about our attitudes—what we allow to take root in our hearts and shape our desires. The things we treasure most reveal much about what truly matters to us.

Read both Mathew 6:19 - 21 & Luke 12:32-34

Matthew speaks about the dangers of storing treasures on earth; being destroyed by moths and rust. Luke says to sell your treasures and give them to the poor.

1. Given these two perspectives, what is God saying about treasures?

____
____
____

Read Exodus 19:1-6

The Israelites had witnessed some powerful and amazing things; the locust, frogs, water turned to blood, the parting of the Red Sea so they could cross on dry land. The Mediterranean Sea, or Red Sea, provides a conduit south through the Suez Canal and Gulf of Suez. This salty sea is just over 190 miles (300 km) across at its widest point, and about 1,200 miles (1,900 km) in length. There's a measured maximum depth of 8,200 feet (2,500 m), and an estimated average depth of 1,640 feet (500 m). Much of the immediate shoreline is quite shallow.

2. What would cause them to doubt and want to go back to Egypt?

____
____
____

3. Have you ever trusted in your own resources rather depend on God?

____
____
____

4. Do you treasure or value your material possessions or your relationship with God?

____
____
____

5. Do you have a relationship with God? If not all you have to do is ask Jesus to come into your life, accept His forgiveness and He will answer you with a resounding YES! (See the prayer for salvation in the Conclusion section)

____
____
____

6. Having witnessed the miracles God performed, shouldn't the Israelites have realized that God was on their side, and had answered their prayers for deliverance?

____
____
____

Read Deuteronomy 8:10-14

7. What is your 'Egypt'; is it your job or career, your money or possessions?

____
____
____

8. What are you 'slave' to? Is it a television show, a drug or addicting habit, sex, and people pleasing?

____
____
____

9. What is being asked and what is being promised?

____
____
____

10. What is your response?

____
____
____

Recognize The Idols in Your Life?

We've come to the final lesson. What a journey it has been! Throughout this study, we have explored the condition of the Heart in our first lesson, examined where our Focus lies in the second lesson, confronted the issue of Greed in the third lesson, and considered our Treasures in the fourth lesson. Now, in our fifth and final lesson, our attention turns to the topic of Idols.

It's easy to think that people today do not have idols in their lives—that idolatry was a practice confined to biblical times. However, I would argue otherwise. To begin with, let's clarify what we mean by idols. According to Webster's Dictionary, idols are defined as follows:

- An image or other material object representing a deity to which religious worship is addressed.
- Bible - an image of a deity other than God. Or - the deity itself
- Any person or thing regarded with blind admiration, adoration, or devotion:
- A mere image or semblance of something, visible but without substance, phantom
- A figment of the mind; fantasy
- A false conception or notion; fallacy

I favor the 2nd definition; "An image of a deity OTHER than God". What does the Bible say about idols? First, let's looks at the 10 commandments; the first three commandments have to do with our relationship with God. In Exodus 20:1-6; *"And God spoke all these words, saying: I am the Lord your God, who brought you out of the land of Egypt, out of the house of bondage. You shall have no other gods before Me. "You shall not make for yourself a carved image—any likeness of anything that is in heaven above, or that is in the earth beneath, or that is in the water under the earth; you shall not bow down to them nor serve them. For I, the Lord your God, am a jealous God, visiting the iniquity of the fathers upon the children to the third and fourth generations of those who hate Me, but showing mercy to thousands, to those who love Me and keep My commandments."*

Modern Idolatry: Recognizing Our Own Idols

God leaves no room for ambiguity—He makes it abundantly clear that He will not tolerate His creation having idols. If we allow idols into our lives, there will be consequences for that choice. To better understand this concept in today's context, let's consider Webster's definition of an idol: "any person or thing regarded with blind admiration, adoration, or devotion." Now, compare this definition to God's commandment: "You shall have no other gods before Me."

Reflecting honestly, would you say you have idols in your life today? If Christians and even non-believers examine themselves truthfully, most would have to admit that idols exist in their lives. However, these idols are not necessarily images as described in the Bible, nor are they associated with pagan worship rituals. In our modern society, we consider ourselves too sophisticated for such practices.

Instead, our idols are often things that appear good, acceptable, or even admirable. They can include our jobs, our families, ministry work, and, quite candidly, our money. It's not just money itself, but the pursuit of making it, spending it, and keeping it that can become an idol in our lives. These things, though not inherently wrong, can easily take the place of God if we are not vigilant, becoming modern forms of idolatry that distract us from our relationship with Him.

Personal Examples of Modern Idolatry

To illustrate what modern idolatry can look like, consider my own life as an example. I recognize that my idols can be computer games and classic black and white TV westerns. For those unfamiliar, television originally aired in black and white before the advent of color broadcasts. I find myself able to spend hours absorbed in watching these westerns or playing games—time that could and should be devoted to engaging with God's Word. This time could be better spent renewing my mind, as Paul encourages, or studying to show myself approved, as well as fulfilling the daily responsibilities that Christians are called to observe.

I continually have to remind myself not to let anything take precedence over God. For other people, idols might take the form of their careers—working 80 or more hours a week, neglecting time with family, skipping time in scripture, or being too preoccupied to attend church and fellowship with other believers.

For some, it might be a focus on physical fitness or appearance. While taking care of your health is important, becoming obsessed with your looks can cross the line into idolatry. Materialism is another common idol in today's culture—owning the best or most expensive items, whether it's Michael Kors, Prada, Gucci, DKNY, or always feeling the need to have the latest and greatest products.

Additionally, technology and electronic gadgets can become idols in our lives. The constant allure of Apple products, iPods, Kindles, and countless other devices promoted by retailers and advertisers can easily capture our attention and devotion.

For the record, classic westerns, computer games, working, exercising, caring about your looks, having the latest technology or purchasing a designer item are not bad things, UNLESS they are put above God; then they become idols. In 2 Kings 17:40-41 the Message Bible puts it this way: *But they didn't pay any attention. They kept doing what they'd always done. As it turned out, all the time these people were putting on a front of worshiping God, they were at the same time involved with their local idols. And they're still doing it. Like father, like son.*

Consequences of Modern Idolatry

This passage highlights that the people were "walking the fence," attempting to worship God on their own terms rather than according to His standards. In reality, many of us can relate to this behavior—we often want to enjoy the benefits of our choices without facing the consequences, essentially wanting to "have our cake and eat it too."

God's Response to Idolatry

So, what are some of the consequences of allowing idols to take priority over God? The Bible is clear: God is a jealous God and will not tolerate being placed second. When we let other things become idols in our lives, God will ensure we are put in situations where our focus is redirected back to Him.

Examples of Consequences

- **Career and Work**: If your job becomes your main source of pride, you may face layoffs or downsizing—especially with the rise of AI. This can shift your focus away from work and encourage greater reliance on God. Suddenly, you have an abundance of time—time that can be used to refocus on God. With a reduced or lost income, you are compelled to rely on Him for your needs.

- **Physical Fitness**: If exercising and physical health are your primary focus, you might suffer a pulled muscle or a severe injury that prevents you from working out for weeks, forcing you to reevaluate your priorities.
- **Entertainment and Hobbies**: If you find yourself absorbed in activities like computer games or watching classic westerns, you may suddenly lose access—perhaps your computer crashes and games are lost, or your internet connection fails, removing these distractions from your life.
- **Money and Possessions**: If money is your idol, you could lose it unexpectedly—an unplanned expense, a repair, or even illness could demand your financial resources, using your money for something other than what you intended.

A Call to Refocus

No matter what form an idol takes, God will get your attention one way or another. He refuses to be ignored or set aside. When we allow anything to come before Him, He permits circumstances to arise that force us to shift our attention back to Him, reminding us that He alone is worthy of our devotion.

You are to tear down your idols and worship God only. Anything that sets itself above God will be brought down. Isaiah 14:12-14 tells of the fallen angel: "*How you are fallen from heaven, O Lucifer, son of the morning! How you are cut down to the ground, You who weakened the nations! For you have said in your heart: **'I will** ascend into heaven, **I will** exalt my throne above the stars of God; **I will** also sit on the mount of the congregation On the farthest sides of the north; **I will** ascend above the heights of the clouds, **I will** be like the Most High.*" (Emphasis added)

The Danger of Pride and Self-Focus

In the passages from Isaiah, the phrase "I will" appears five times, emphasizing the self-centered attitude that led to Lucifer's fall. This repeated focus on personal ambition—saying, "I need to…," "I have to…," "I'm going to…," and referring to "my this or my that"—reveals a mindset centered on self and personal desires. When life becomes all about what we want, pride takes root.

Pride as an Idol

Pride itself becomes an idol when it occupies our thoughts and actions. As Webster's Dictionary defines pride, it is "a false conception or notion; fallacy." This false sense of self-importance stands in direct opposition to the worship of God.

Worshiping God Wholeheartedly

The way to tear down idols—especially the idol of pride—is by worshiping God with all our heart, mind, and soul. When we make God the center of our lives, every idol loses its hold. Putting God first in everything we do is the key to overcoming pride and other distractions.

Practical Steps to Refocus on God

- Spend time in God's Word daily.
- Set aside quiet time for prayer and reflection.
- Fellowship with other believers to build spiritual strength.
- Turn off the TV and unplug the phone to eliminate distractions.
- Look for God's presence in His creation—flowers, trees, rivers, lakes, and mountains.
- Thank, praise, and worship God, recognizing His majesty and worthiness.

As we take these steps, we learn to see God's hand in every aspect of life and respond with gratitude and worship. He alone is worthy to be praised.

Key Points from the Guide:

- Stewardship is about seeing everything—possessions, opportunities, relationships—as gifts from God.
- Responding with gratitude means recognizing God's provision and expressing thanks in both words and actions.
- Worship flows from a heart that acknowledges God's sovereignty and goodness in all circumstances.

Practical Application:

- As you dedicate your home, resources, and daily life to God, you become a living testimony of His grace.
- Gratitude and worship are not just responses—they are ongoing attitudes that shape how you live and interact with others.

Can You Recognize the Idols in Your Life? - Bible Study Lesson

Introduction
Identifying and Addressing Idols in Your Life

The question of whether Adam and Eve's sin was the first sin, or if pride itself was the original sin, prompts us to reflect on the nature of pride. Pride occurs when we place ourselves above God and others, elevating our own desires and perspectives above what God intends for us.

This reflection leads us to consider the idols present in our own lives. Idols are not always physical objects; they can be anything—possessions, ambitions, relationships, habits—that take precedence over God in our hearts and actions. Recognizing these idols requires honesty, both with ourselves and with God. While God already knows what occupies our hearts, it is our responsibility to identify these idols and respond as He reveals them to us.

Once we have recognized the idols in our lives, the next step is repentance—turning away from anything that has taken God's rightful place. Removing these idols is an ongoing process, guided by God's grace and direction. As we confront these areas, we invite God to reclaim His place in every aspect of our lives, growing in humility and dependence on Him.

Read Romans 12:2

1. Are you conforming to the patterns of this world?

____

____

____

2. If so, what can you do about it? What or who do you need to remove from your life?

____

____

____

Read Psalm 115:4

3. What idols do we have in the 21st Century that could fit the description of silver and gold?

____

____

____

4. Based on what you've learned so far in this series, how does God respond to being replaced by idols in any form?

____

____

____

Read Daniel 4:28-32

5. What does this passage say about pride? To fully understand the story read the entire chapter. Early in the chapter King Nebuchadnezzar had a dream which Daniel interrupted. Do you suppose the king forgot what was told to him?

6. What would you say are some idols in your life today?

7. What do you need to do to remove them?

8. What can you do to prevent idols forming in your life?

Read 2 Chronicles 7:14

9. What do you need to repent concerning; your heart, your focus, greed, treasures, or idols?

Read 2 Corinthians 6:16

10. What is your response?

Examples of Stewardship in Daily Life

1. Managing Finances Wisely

- Budgeting and spending responsibly, recognizing that all resources ultimately belong to God.
- Giving generously—tithing or supporting charitable causes and those in need

2. Using Your Home for Ministry

- Hosting small group Bible studies or gatherings to encourage spiritual growth and fellowship.
- Welcoming friends, neighbors, or colleagues for meals, using hospitality as a way to witness and share God's love

3. Time Management

- Prioritizing time for prayer, worship, and studying scripture.
- Volunteering in your church or community, serving others with your time and talents.

4. Talents and Skills

- Using your professional skills to help others, such as mentoring, teaching, or providing services to those who cannot afford them.
- Participating in church ministries or outreach programs that align with your gifts.

5. Caring for Creation

- Practicing environmental stewardship by recycling, conserving energy, and caring for the world God created.

6. Relationships

- Investing in family and friendships, modeling godly behavior and encouragement.
  Forgiving others and seeking reconciliation, reflecting Christ's love in your interactions.

7. Personal Growth

- Continually seeking to grow in faith, character, and wisdom.
- Being accountable to others and open to correction, striving to be a faithful steward in all areas of life.

Conclusion

This study is not intended to make you feel inadequate or pass judgment on you. The Bible teaches us in Romans 8:1 that there is no condemnation for those who are in Christ Jesus. As the saying goes, when we know better, we do better. With that in mind, let's take a moment to review the key points we've discussed:

- Watch where your Heart is
- Watch what you Focus on
- Watch and be aware of areas of Greed in your life
- Watch what you Treasure
- Watch what and who are your Idols

A Call to Wholehearted Commitment

God does not desire your wealth or possessions; rather, He seeks your heart, your obedience, and your reverence. As Christians, we are called to stand apart—to be different, unique, and special in the world. If you find yourself ensnared by worldly pursuits, it can hinder you from becoming the person God intends you to be.

To fulfill God's purpose, commit yourself to honoring Him, diligently studying His Word, and faithfully stewarding everything He has entrusted to you.

An Invitation to Faith

If you are not yet a member of the Body of Christ, these principles may not resonate with you. However, you have the opportunity to accept Jesus as the Lord of your life. You can do this by praying the following simple prayer:

"Dear God, I want to be a part of your family. You said in Your Word that if I acknowledge that You raised Jesus from the dead and I asked for forgiveness of my sins and accept Him as my Lord and Savior, I would be saved. So God, I now say that I believe You raised Jesus from the dead and that He is alive and well. I accept Him now as my personal Lord and Savior. I accept the gift of salvation from sin right now. I am now saved from the penalty of sin. Jesus is my Lord. Jesus is my Savior. Thank you, Father God, for forgiving me, saving me, and giving me eternal life with You. Amen!"

Next Steps for New Believers

If you prayed this prayer for the first time, it is important to share this decision with someone you trust. Sharing your new faith marks the beginning of your journey as a believer and provides encouragement and support as you grow.

To nurture your relationship with God and understand His purpose for your life, seek out a Bible-based church where you can connect with other Christians, receive sound teaching, and participate in a supportive community. Through fellowship and regular study of God's Word, you will come to know the God of the Universe more deeply and discover the unique purpose He has for your life.

Welcome to the Family!

Biblical References

Introduction

Psalms 24:1-3 - The earth is the LORD's, and everything in it, the world, and all who live in it; for he founded it on the seas and established it on the waters. Who may ascend the mountain of the LORD? Who may stand in his holy place?"

Matthew 25:15 - And to one he gave five talents, to another two, and to another one, to each according to his own ability; and immediately he went on a journey."

Matthew 25:29 - For to everyone who has, more will be given and he will have abundance; but from him who does not have, even what he has will be taken away."

Deuteronomy 8:18b - But remember the Lord your God, for it is he who gives you the ability to produce wealth,"

Genesis 13:2 - Abram had become very wealthy in livestock and in silver and gold

Psalms. 1:3 - That person is like a tree planted by streams of water, which yields its fruit in season and whose leaf does not wither— whatever they do prospers.

Psalms 112:1-3 - 1 Praise the Lord. Blessed are those who fear the Lord, who find great delight in his commands 2 Their children will be mighty in the land; the generation of the upright will be blessed. 3 Wealth and riches are in their houses, and their righteousness endures forever.

1 Timothy 6:17 - Command those who are rich in this present world not to be arrogant nor to put their hope in wealth, which is so uncertain, but to put their hope in God, who richly provides us with everything for our enjoyment.

Matters of the Heart

Jeremiah 17:1-10 - "Judah's sin is engraved with an iron tool, inscribed with a flint point, on the tablets of their hearts and on the horns of their altars. 2 Even their children remember their altars and Asherah poles beside the spreading trees and on the high hills. 3 My mountain in the land and your wealth and all your treasures I will give away as plunder, together with your high places, because of sin throughout your country. 4 Through your own fault you will lose the inheritance I gave you. I will enslave you to your enemies in a land you do not know, for you have kindled my anger, and it will burn forever."5 This is what the Lord says: "Cursed is the one who trusts in man, who draws strength from mere flesh and whose heart turns away from the Lord. 6 That person will be like a bush in the wastelands; they will not see prosperity when it comes. They will dwell in the parched places of the desert, in a salt land where no one lives. 7 "But blessed is the one who trusts in the Lord, whose confidence is in him. 8 They will be like a tree planted by the water that sends out its roots by the stream. It does not fear when heat comes; its leaves are always green. It has no worries in a year of drought and never fails to bear fruit." 9 The heart is deceitful above all things and beyond cure. Who can understand it? 10 "I the Lord search the heart and examine the mind, to reward each person according to their conduct, according to what their deeds deserve."

Romans 8:27 - Now He who searches the hearts knows what the mind of the Spirit is, because He makes intercession for the saints according to the will of God.

3 John 3:4 - I have no greater joy than to hear that my children are walking in the truth.

Psalm 37:4 - Take delight in the Lord, and he will give you the desires of your heart

Acts 16:16-28 - 16 Once when we were going to the place of prayer, we were met by a female slave who had a spirit by which she predicted the future. She earned a great deal of money for her owners by fortune-telling. 17 She followed Paul and the rest of us, shouting, “These men are servants of the Most High God, who are telling you the way to be saved.” 18 She kept this up for many days. Finally Paul became so annoyed that he turned around and said to the spirit, “In the name of Jesus Christ I command you to come out of her!” At that moment the spirit left her. 19 When her owners realized that their hope of making money was gone, they seized Paul and Silas and dragged them into the marketplace to face the authorities. 20 They brought them before the magistrates and said, “These men are Jews, and are throwing our city into an uproar 21 by advocating customs unlawful for us Romans to accept or practice.” 22 The crowd joined in the attack against Paul and Silas, and the magistrates ordered them to be stripped and beaten with rods. 23 After they had been severely flogged, they were thrown into prison, and the jailer was commanded to guard them carefully. 24 When he received these orders, he put them in the inner cell and fastened their feet in the stocks.

25 About midnight Paul and Silas were praying and singing hymns to God, and the other prisoners were listening to them. 26 Suddenly there was such a violent earthquake that the foundations of the prison were shaken. At once all the prison doors flew open, and everyone’s chains came loose. 27 The jailer woke up, and when he saw the prison doors open, he drew his sword and was about to kill himself because he thought the prisoners had escaped. 28 But Paul shouted, “Don’t harm yourself! We are all here!”

1 Timothy 6:10 - For the love of money is a root of all kinds of evil, for which some have strayed from the faith in their greediness, and pierced themselves through with many sorrows

1 Timothy 6:6 - Now godliness with contentment is great gain

Matthew 6:33 - But seek first the kingdom of God and His righteousness, and all these things shall be added to you.

Matthew 6:32 - For after all these things the Gentiles seek. For your heavenly Father knows that you need all these things.

Proverbs 21:15 - It is a joy for the just to do justice, But destruction will come to the workers of iniquity.

Isaiah 12:3 - Therefore with joy you will draw water From the wells of salvation.

Romans 12:2 - And do not be conformed to this world, but be transformed by the renewing of your mind, that you may prove what is that good and acceptable and perfect will of God.

3 John 1:4 - I have no greater joy than to hear that my children walk in truth.

Acts 16:25 - But at midnight Paul and Silas were praying and singing hymns to God, and the prisoners were listening to them.

1 Corinthians 2:16 - For "who has known the mind of the Lord that he may instruct Him?" But we have the mind of Christ

Psalm 19:14 - Let the words of my mouth and the meditation of my heart Be acceptable in Your sight, O Lord, my strength and my Redeemer.

What's Your Focus?

Psalm 86:11 - Teach me your way, Lord, that I may rely on your faithfulness; give me an undivided heart, that I may fear your name."

Jeremiah 29:11 - For I know the plans I have for you, declares the Lord, plans to prosper you and not to harm you, plans to give you hope and a future.

Romans 8:5-6 - 5 Those who live according to the flesh have their minds set on what the flesh desires; but those who live in accordance with the Spirit have their minds set on what the Spirit desires. 6 The mind governed by the flesh is death, but the mind governed by the Spirit is life and peace.

Exodus 16:15-17; 19-20 - And Moses said to them, "This is the bread which the Lord has given you to eat. 16 This is the thing which the Lord has commanded: 'Let every man gather it according to each one's need, one omer for each person, according to the number of persons; let every man take for those who are in his tent.'" 19 And Moses said, "Let no one leave any of it till morning." 20 Notwithstanding they did not heed Moses. But some of them left part of it until morning, and it bred worms and stank.

Exodus 16:16 - Then the Lord said to Moses, "How long will you refuse to keep my commands and my instructions?

Malachi 3:7-9 - 7 Ever since the time of your ancestors you have turned away from my decrees and have not kept them. Return to me, and I will return to you," says the Lord Almighty. "But you ask, 'How are we to return?' 8 "Will a mere mortal rob God? Yet you rob me. "But you ask, 'How are we robbing you?' "In tithes and offerings. 9 You are under a curse—your whole nation—because you are robbing me.

Genesis 14:18-20 – 18 Then Melchizedek king of Salem brought out bread and wine; he was the priest of God Most High. 19 And he blessed him and said: "Blessed be Abram of God Most High, Possessor of heaven and earth; 20 And blessed be God Most High, Who has delivered your enemies into your hand." And he gave him a tithe of all.

2 Corinthians 10:5 - We demolish arguments and every pretension that sets itself up against the knowledge of God, and we take captive every thought to make it obedient to Christ.

Proverbs 12:15 - The way of a fool is right in his own eyes, but he who listens to counsel is wise.

Deuteronomy 11:18 - Fix these words of mine in your hearts and minds; tie them as symbols on your hands and bind them on your foreheads.

Colossians 3:1-3 - 1 Since, then, you have been raised with Christ, set your hearts on things above, where Christ is, seated at the right hand of God. 2 Set your minds on things above, not on earthly things. 3 For you died, and your life is now hidden with Christ in God.

Romans 12:2 - And do not be conformed to this world, but be transformed by the renewing of your mind, that you may prove what is that good and acceptable and perfect will of God.

2 Chronicles 7:14 - if my people, who are called by my name, will humble themselves and pray and seek my face and turn from their wicked ways, then I will hear from heaven, and I will forgive their sin and will heal their land.

Is Greed Good or Bad?

Matthew 19:16-22 - 16 Just then a man came up to Jesus and asked, "Teacher, what good thing must I do to get eternal life?" 17 "Why do you ask me about what is good?" Jesus replied. "There is only One who is good. If you want to enter life, keep the commandments."18 "Which ones?" he inquired. Jesus replied, "'You shall not murder, you shall not commit adultery, you shall not steal, you shall not give false testimony, 19 honor your father and mother,' and 'love your neighbor as yourself.' 20 "All these I have kept," the young man said. "What do I still lack?" 21 Jesus answered, "If you want to be perfect, go, sell your possessions and give to the poor, and you will have treasure in heaven. Then come, follow me." 22 When the young man heard this, he went away sad, because he had great wealth.

Matthew 19:23 - Then Jesus said to his disciples, "Truly I tell you, it is hard for someone who is rich to enter the kingdom of heaven".

Luke 12:13-19 - 13 Someone in the crowd said to him, "Teacher, tell my brother to divide the inheritance with me." 14 Jesus replied, "Man, who appointed me a judge or an arbiter between you?" 15 Then he said to them, "Watch out! Be on your guard against all kinds of greed; life does not consist in an abundance of possessions." 16 And he told them this parable: "The ground of a certain rich man yielded an abundant harvest. 17 He thought to himself, 'What shall I do? I have no place to store my crops.' 18 "Then he said, 'This is what I'll do. I will tear down my barns and build bigger ones, and there I will store my surplus grain. 19 And I'll say to myself, "You have plenty of grain laid up for many years. Take life easy; eat, drink and be merry."'

1 Timothy 6:6-10 - 6 But godliness with contentment is great gain. 7 For we brought nothing into the world, and we can take nothing out of it. 8 But if we have food and clothing, we will be content with that. 9 Those who want to get rich fall into temptation and a trap and into many foolish and harmful desires that plunge people into ruin and destruction. 10 For the love of money is a root of all kinds of evil. Some people, eager for money, have wandered from the faith and pierced themselves with many griefs.

Proverbs 23:17 - Do not let your heart envy sinners, But be zealous for the fear of the Lord all the day;

Ecclesiastes 5:13 - I have seen a grievous evil under the sun: wealth hoarded to the harm of its owners…

What Do You Treasure?

Mathew 6:19 - 21 - 19 "Do not store up for yourselves treasures on earth, where moths and vermin destroy, and where thieves break in and steal. 20 But store up for yourselves treasures in heaven, where moths and vermin do not destroy, and where thieves do not break in and steal. 21 For where your treasure is, there your heart will be also.

Luke 12:32-34 - 32 “Do not be afraid, little flock, for your Father has been pleased to give you the kingdom. 33 Sell your possessions and give to the poor. Provide purses for yourselves that will not wear out, a treasure in heaven that will never fail, where no thief comes near and no moth destroys. 34 For where your treasure is, there your heart will be also.

Exodus 19:1- 6 - 1 On the first day of the third month after the Israelites left Egypt—on that very day—they came to the Desert of Sinai. 2 After they set out from Rephidim, they entered the Desert of Sinai, and Israel camped there in the desert in front of the mountain. 3 Then Moses went up to God, and the Lord called to him from the mountain and said, “This is what you are to say to the descendants of Jacob and what you are to tell the people of Israel: 4 ‘You yourselves have seen what I did to Egypt, and how I carried you on eagles’ wings and brought you to myself. 5 Now if you obey me fully and keep my covenant, then out of all nations you will be my treasured possession. Although the whole earth is mine, 6 you will be for me a kingdom of priests and a holy nation.’ These are the words you are to speak to the Israelites.”

Deuteronomy 8:10-14 - 10 When you have eaten and are satisfied, praise the Lord your God for the good land he has given you. 11 Be careful that you do not forget the Lord your God, failing to observe his commands, his laws and his decrees that I am giving you this day. 12 Otherwise, when you eat and are satisfied, when you build fine houses and settle down, 13 and when your herds and flocks grow large and your silver and gold increase and all you have is multiplied, 14 then your heart will become proud and you will forget the Lord your God, who brought you out of Egypt, out of the land of slavery.

Can You Recognize The Idols In Your Life?

Exodus 20:1-6 And God spoke all these words, saying: 2 “I am the Lord your God, who brought you out of the land of Egypt, out of the house of bondage. 3 “You shall have no other gods before Me. 4 “You shall not make for yourself a carved image—any likeness of anything that is in heaven above, or that is in the earth beneath, or that is in the water under the earth; 5 you shall not bow down to them nor serve them. For I, the Lord your God, am a jealous God, visiting the iniquity of the fathers upon the children to the third and fourth generations of those who hate Me, 6 but showing mercy to thousands, to those who love Me and keep My commandments.

Ephesians 4:22-24 22 that you put off, concerning your former conduct, the old man which grows corrupt according to the deceitful lusts, 23 and be renewed in the spirit of your mind, 24 and that you put on the new man which was created according to God, in true righteousness and holiness.

Isaiah 14:12-14 - 12 “How you are fallen from heaven, O Lucifer, son of the morning! How you are cut down to the ground, You who weakened the nations! 13 For you have said in your heart: ‘I will ascend into heaven, I will exalt my throne above the stars of God; I will also sit on the mount of the congregation On the farthest sides of the north; 14 I will ascend above the heights of the clouds, I will be like the Most High.’

Romans 12:2 - Do not conform to the pattern of this world, but be transformed by the renewing of your mind. Then you will be able to test and approve what God’s will is—his good, pleasing and perfect will.

2 Timothy 2:15 - 15 Study and do your best to present yourself to God approved, a workman [tested by trial] who has no reason to be ashamed, accurately handling and skillfully teaching the word of truth.

Psalm 115:4 - Their idols are silver and gold, The work of men's hands

Daniel 4:28-32 - 28 All this came upon King Nebuchadnezzar. 29 At the end of the twelve months he was walking about the royal palace of Babylon. 30 The king spoke, saying, "Is not this great Babylon, that I have built for a royal dwelling by my mighty power and for the honor of my majesty?"
31 While the word was still in the king's mouth, a voice fell from heaven: "King Nebuchadnezzar, to you it is spoken: the kingdom has departed from you! 32 And they shall drive you from men, and your dwelling shall be with the beasts of the field. They shall make you eat grass like oxen; and seven times shall pass over you, until you know that the Most High rules in the kingdom of men, and gives it to whomever He chooses."

2 Chronicles 7:14 - if My people who are called by My name will humble themselves, and pray and seek My face, and turn from their wicked ways, then I will hear from heaven, and will forgive their sin and heal their land.

2 Corinthians 6:16 - 16 What agreement is there between the temple of God and idols? For we are the temple of the living God. As God has said: "I will live with them and walk among them, and I will be their God, and they will be my people."

Conclusion

Romans 8:1 - Therefore, there is now no condemnation for those who are in Christ Jesus

Resources

Barboza, D., & Warren, A. (2002, February 25). At Enron, Lavish Excess Often Came Before Success. Retrieved August 17, 2014

"Cats in the Cradle" Artist: Harry Chapin, Album: Verities & Balderdash, Released: 1974

Johnson, B. T. (2016). Pharisees. In J. D. Barry, D. Bomar, D. R. Brown, R. Klippenstein, D. Mangum, C. Sinclair Wolcott, … W. Widder (Eds.), The Lexham Bible Dictionary. Bellingham, WA: Lexham Press

Jones, T. H. (1996). David. In D. R. W. Wood, I. H. Marshall, A. R. Millard, J. I. Packer, & D. J. Wiseman (Eds.), New Bible dictionary (3rd ed., p. 260). Leicester, England; Downers Grove, IL: InterVarsity Press

Knox, D. B. (1996). Wealth. In D. R. W. Wood, I. H. Marshall, A. R. Millard, J. I. Packer, & D. J. Wiseman (Eds.), New Bible dictionary (3rd ed., p. 1233). Leicester, England; Downers Grove, IL: InterVarsity Press

Mallon, B. (2013, July 12). Divorce Study: Financial Arguments Early In Relationship May Predict Divorce. Retrieved August 17, 2014, from http://www.huffingtonpost.com/2013/07/12/divorce-study_n_3587811.html

Manser, M. H. (2009). Dictionary of Bible Themes: The Accessible and Comprehensive Tool for Topical Studies. London: Martin Manser

Matthew Henry's Commentary; Chapter 6:6-12

Prison, Prisoners and the Bible, A Paper Delivered to "Breaking Down the Walls Conference" by Dr Christopher D. Marshall* Tyndale Graduate School of Theology, Auckland retrieved from http://www.restorativejustice.org/10fulltext/marshall-christopher.-prison-prisoners-and-the-bible/

The Only Definition of Success That Matters, by Jeff Haden, July 28, 2012, retrieved from http://www.inc.com/jeff-haden/the-only-definition-of-success-that-matters.html

The Sermon on the Mount, By: Brian Schwertley, retrieved from http://www.reformedonline.com/view/reformedonline/sermononmount1.htm

Read more at http://www.brainyquote.com/citation/quotes/quotes/s/samuelbutl122806.html#eo0f4GIOMo6fcYht.99

Samuel Butler. (n.d.). BrainyQuote.com. Retrieved August 17, 2014, from BrainyQuote.com Web site: http://www.brainyquote.com/quotes/quotes/s/samuelbutl122806.html

Source: Israel Ministry of Foreign Affairs, Copyright 2012 The American-Israeli Cooperative Enterprise retrieved from http://www.jewishvirtuallibrary.org/jsource/History/Romans.html

Wall Street (1987), Director: Oliver Stone, Writers: Stanley Weiser, Oliver Stone

Notes

Printed in Dunstable, United Kingdom

91218268R00036